CHOOSE YOUR OWN ADVENTURE®

Kids Love Reading
Choose Your Own Adventure®!

"I like the way you can choose the way
the story goes."
Beckett Kahn, age 7

"If you don't read this book, you'll get payback."
Amy Cook, age 8½

"I thought this book was funny.
I think younger and older kids will like it."
Tessa Jernigan, age 6½

"This is fun reading. Once you go in to have an
adventure, you may never come out."
Jude Fidel, age 7

Illustrated by Keith Newton
Book design by Stacey Boyd, Big Eyedea Visual Design
For information regarding permission, write to:

CHOOSECO
P.O. Box 46
Waitsfield, Vermont 05673
www.cyoa.com

A DRAGONLARK BOOK

ISBN: 1-937133-27-3
EAN: 978-1-937133-27-6

Published simultaneously in the United States and Canada

Printed in China

9 8 7 6 5 4 3 2 1

CHOOSE YOUR OWN ADVENTURE®

YOUR GRANDPARENTS ARE NINJAS

BY ANSON MONTGOMERY

A DRAGONLARK BOOK

To Karen Ortega, Abuela to many. Thank you!

READ THIS FIRST!!!

WATCH OUT!
THIS BOOK IS DIFFERENT
from every book you've ever read.

Do not read this book from the first page
through to the last page.
Instead, start on page 1 and read until you
come to your first choice. Then turn to the
page shown and see what happens.

When you come to the end of a story,
you can go back and start again.
Every choice leads to a new adventure.

Good luck!

"The bride is here," a large man in a dark suit and sunglasses says into an earpiece. He turns to you and says, "Go to Staging Area One. It's go time!"

"Roger that," you say crisply, standing up straight. "I'll check the route again."

Your grandparents are ninjas. More on that later. You are helping them host a wedding at their inn in the country. Grandma Ami and Grandpa PawPaw met in ninja school in Japan a long time ago. The bride, "The Princess of J-Pop," is internationally famous. Her real name is Akiko Yosano and she is marrying a rich man named Reo Abe. Reo bought Akiko the world's largest diamond as a wedding present. It's almost as big as a baseball. Magazine publishers have offered a $1 million reward for photos of the wedding. Photographers are swarming at the gates. It has been busy all week, but today is crazy!

Turn to the next page.

You walk down the path to Staging Area One, or the bride's tent. The inn is beautiful every day, but today feels magical. Flowers are everywhere. A pink carriage waits on the path leading from the main house.

The white horses' coats are blinding in the sun. Flags and kites fill the sky above, and the gardens are filled with guests eating small sandwiches and having lemonade.

Turn to page 5.

You reach the bride's tent.

"Help! Somebody help!" a voice yells from inside the tent. "The jewels are gone!" This sounds very serious. You look at the guard outside the tent. He knows you are the grandchild of the innkeepers, and he nods at you as he runs in.

You run after the guard and scan the inside of the tent.

"I came out and it was gone! All of it! Look!" Kioko, one of the four bridesmaids, tells the guard. She points to a table with a velvet tablecloth with a jewelry box on it. Behind the table, someone has cut a hole in the tent.

"They must have cut through the back and taken the jewels! I'll stay here," the guard says to you. "You go through the hole and see what you can find."

Turn to the next page.

"First I need to know what the jewels were in," you say.

"They were in a black briefcase. It has a fingerprint lock on it. Only Akiko can open it," Kioko says.

"Gotcha," you say.

"Hurry, get going!" the guard says, pointing at the hole in the tent.

You dive after the trail of the thief. Why are you the one who has to push through the prickly hedge behind the tent? Probably because your grandparents are ninjas and everyone knows you are a ninja-in-training, or "Baby Ninja," as Grandpa PawPaw calls you.

"Watch where you're going!" someone yells from the other side of the hedge.

Turn to page 8.

"Is this the one, dear?" Grandma asks you.

"The one what?" the woman asks. "What do you think we've done?!"

"The one who stole the jewels! Where are they?" you demand dramatically.

"What are you talking about? What happened to the jewels?" the manager asks. "Don't tell me yet another disaster! Just after I learned that my assistant, Yukio here, told *HelloPeopleToday!* magazine about the wedding vows."

"But you said that it would be, quote: 'great if the whole world knew that The Princess of J-Pop was releasing her wedding vows as her next single!' That's what you said!" Yukio snaps.

"But I didn't mean for *us* to be the ones! You know she wants to keep it all a secret until after the wedding!"

"But why were you running away if you didn't do anything wrong?" you ask.

Turn to page 22.

Through the prickly hedge and next to the dove pool, one of the waiters for the wedding walks with a heavy tray of juice drinks.

Go on to the next page.

A person dressed all in blue dashes toward him, knocking him and the tray to the ground!

Then the person in blue runs and ducks between tents, vanishing. You can't see their face. You rush to help the waiter up, but he pushes you away.

"Stop that maniac!" the waiter screams.

Do you follow after the person who pushed the waiter down and ran away? Maybe it was the Jewel Ninja, the notorious jewel thief? Who else would be running like that?

Or do you follow the prickly hedge toward the maze? You're only a Baby Ninja! What would Grandma Ami or Grandpa PawPaw do?

If you decide to go after the running person, turn to the next page.

If you push through the hedge and into the maze, turn to page 16.

You round the corner of the tent and follow the person wearing blue into the kitchen. You are both running fast.

The kitchen smells wonderful.

Platters of glistening sashimi and sushi are laid out in beautiful patterns. Tables piled high with cheese look like small mountains. Your stomach growls. But you need to stay focused!

"They went that way!" screams the head chef. She has a fancy hat on her head, and she is pointing with the largest, sharpest looking knife you have ever seen. "Up the stairs! If anyone messes with my wedding cake, protect it with your life!"

Turn to page 12.

Passing up all of the delicious food, you run up the back stairs.

"Protect the cake, the cake!" you hear the chef yell from below.

You run up the stairs as fast as you can, but the person in blue has vanished. You look down a long hallway with doors to different rooms where most of the guests are staying. There! A door halfway down the hall creaks as it starts to close. You run down the hall when you hear someone yelling from the other direction.

"Raccoon alert!! Raccoon alert! Help! Help!"

A raccoon in the inn! This could ruin the wedding.

If you try to get to the door before it closes, turn to page 32.

If you decide that the "Raccoon Alert" is more important, turn to page 33.

"We'll tell the security team and see if we can follow the trail. She has to be on the property somewhere. We'll find her and the jewels!"

You and Grandpa tell the security team, and they spread out, looking for the Jewel Ninja. Grandpa helps them through the maze, but they turn up nothing.

"We still have a few hours before the wedding, kiddo," Grandpa says to you in a kind voice. "Why don't we take a break and head down to the barn and see if we can help get the horses ready?"

"Okay," you say glumly, disappointed that you were the one who let the Jewel Ninja go.

You follow Grandpa PawPaw to the big barn.

The carriage sits outside. Four huge white horses stand in front. The carriage driver helps you curry the horses and feed them carrots.

Turn to the next page.

As you are finishing, a young man with spiky hair holding a microphone approaches the carriage. A man and woman with news cameras are not far behind him.

Go on to the next page.

"JAM Entertainment News! Sir or Madam!" the guy with the microphone and spiky hair says. "What do you think about the wedding? Who's fighting? Who's feeling the itchy bite of the love bug in the air?"

"Sorry, folks, this is a private wedding, and I'll have to ask you to leave," Grandpa says politely but firmly. He is carrying a water bucket yoke. Both buckets are filled to the brim.

Turn to page 24.

The prickly hedge wall is a part of the very big maze at the center of your grandparents' property. They made it when they moved in and built the inn, many years ago.

Youch! Thorns and branches tear at you as you push your way through. You can tell someone else just crashed through by the broken twigs.

Look! Right there on that branch! A scrap of cloth!

You stop in the middle of the hedge and pick up the torn piece of dark blue fabric. It's stretchy, like a bathing suit or workout clothing.

You stick the fabric in your pocket and keep moving. Kioko only yelled for your help about one minute ago, so the jewel thief may still be close by.

Turn to page 18.

18

You burst through the hedge and onto the big lawn, where wedding guests are playing croquet on the green grass.

"Did you see anyone come through here?" you ask the players.

"*Yooooooo-hooooooo!* I saw someone!" shouts a woman with purple hair. She is wearing a Victorian dress and big, dark sunglasses. "They ruined our game! I was just about to win." She speaks very slowly, in a loud, high voice.

"Where did they go?" you ask. "Hurry! Tell me fast!"

"They went into the maze," answers a young man dressed in a silvery tuxedo and top hat, pointing to the entrance to the middle of the hedge maze.

Turn to page 21.

Great.

You run into the center of the maze. The hedges here reach high above your head. You know the maze by heart, but that does not help much if you don't know where the thief went.

Still, you run, making choices at random.

You turn the corner, and there among the marble statues, you find a woman in a dark blue bodysuit with a black briefcase.

"You're trapped, thief!" you yell. "That balcony overlooks a forty-foot cliff!"

"Oh, crackerjacks!" the woman in the bodysuit says.

"Put down the briefcase, now!"

"Or what, Baby Ninja? Grandma and Grandpa aren't here to help you. Tell you what. I'll put down the case if you'll let me by. Otherwise I'll throw it into the river. It is a long way down," she says.

Turn to page 29.

"I ran because I was soaked!" Yukio yells dramatically. She wriggles up from under Grandma's foot. (She lets her go.) "That waiter ran right into me. Look at me!" Yukio says.

"So you didn't steal the jewels?" you ask.

"No! Of course not. We would protect those jewels with our lives."

"I don't think they are the jewel thieves," you admit.

You look at Grandma Ami. She shrugs. You shrug back.

She lets the manager go, then says, "*Gokigen'yō!*"

She throws a tiny glass bottle to the ground. It cracks open. A huge cloud of purple smoke billows up and you all cough.

When you stop coughing, Grandma is gone.

The manager asks, between choking coughs, "What just happened?"

You don't really know.

The End

"We've heard reports that the Jewel Ninja bragged online that she could steal Akiko's tiara right off her head. What do you think of that?"

"I suggest you move along. Last warning," Grandpa says.

"What about the rumors that bad boy Akira from the pop group Teen Heartthrob Go! was seen with Akiko's sister Liyanna? Our viewers want to know!"

One of the other reporters stumbles forward and crashes. His small digital camera drops into the bucket of water with a *plop!*

"Whoops, sorry 'bout that," Grandpa says, not sounding sorry at all. "I'll escort you two out while I get more water from the spring. Wait a sec. Where'd your friend go?" The second camerawoman is nowhere to be seen.

Go on to the next page.

"This changes things. We can't let her film the wedding. I'm going to need some help. You in?" Grandpa asks you.

"Yes!" you say, pulling Grandpa down so you can whisper in his ear, "I think the reporter who disappeared might be the Jewel Ninja! I saw a piece of clothing sticking out of her jacket that was the same color as this cloth that the thief dropped!" You hold up the scrap of dark blue fabric so he can see it.

"Great, you can either drive the carriage to the house to tell your Grandma that we have a lead on the Jewel Ninja. Or you can help me with these two, then we'll go looking together!"

If you choose to drive the carriage to let Grandma and the security team know what is happening, turn to the next page.

If you decide to help Grandpa with the reporters and then look for the thief together, turn to page 48.

You think Grandma should know what's going on right away, so you get in the carriage and head toward the inn.

The horses know the way and *clomp clomp* down the path excitedly. Sophie, who cares for the horses, sits beside you in the carriage.

Go on to the next page.

You turn away from the barn and come upon the four bridesmaids on the path. They all wear fancy dresses. You recognize Kioko from the bride's tent, along with Akiko's sister, Liyanna, who wears leaf and jungle green, her cousin, who wears red, and her best friend, Miko, who wears yellow and orange.

Turn to the next page.

They wave their hands for you to stop.

"Help us, please! And watch the dust!" says Kioko, as Sophie reins the horses in. "We need a ride back to the ceremony. Akiko forgot her veil back at the tent."

"And then the car broke down!" adds Liyanna.

"Can you take us in the carriage? The ceremony is close by, and we were supposed to be there thirty minutes ago!" says Miko.

You look at Sophie. She shrugs.

"Show me the veil, please," you ask the bridesmaid in blue.

"Fine, here you go!" she says, pulling a long, white veil from her purse. The tiny jewels in it glint in the sunlight.

"Hop in," you say, and they climb into the carriage.

"You shouldn't have flashed the veil around," Miko whispers. "You know how much that thing is worth and the Jewel Ninja is still on the loose."

Turn to page 31.

"Who knows how long it will take to find them, if ever? Certainly, not in time for the wedding today. How about letting me go?" the jewel thief continues.

You do wish Grandma or Grandpa were here. They would definitely know what to do! You can't just let the thief go. But you also can't let her throw the jewels into the river! Maybe you could rush forward and grab the case?

If you decide to make a deal to let the thief go in return for the case of jewels, turn to page 44.

If you try to grab the case before she can throw it in the river, turn to page 45.

"I had no choice," she says.

The rest of the drive is uneventful—beautiful even. The bridesmaids talk and laugh. The sun is high when you pull into the parking lot. None of the valets is around.

"Hello. Bridesmaids here," you yell out.

"How perfect," says a person dressed in dark blue, stepping out from between two cars.

"The Jewel Ninja," cries one of the bridesmaids.

"Hand over the veil. It's the last piece I need to complete the heist," says the Jewel Ninja.

Four more ninjas step out into the parking lot. One has a pair of *nunchucks*, one a *sai*, another a *bo* staff, and the fourth holds *shuriken*, or throwing stars.

Turn to page 52.

You run as fast as you can, but the door closes with a loud *CLICK!* before you can stop it.

You put your ear up to the door to see if you can hear anything. You hear two people arguing.

"If Akiko finds out, you'll never be forgiven!" says one voice.

"I know," says another. "Just be quiet and no one will ever find out it was us."

"What do you mean, us? I was never part of the plan!"

"Too late now. Help me change! I'm covered in juice."

Someone taps you on the shoulder and you jump.

Turn to page 34.

"Raccoon alert! In the Garden View Room. Hurry."

You race to the Garden View Room, just next to the ballroom where the reception will be after the ceremony. It has tall glass windows and doors and a fountain, and is kept humid for Grandpa's bonsai plants.

You pull open the Garden View Room's heavy glass doors. Grandma Ami is right behind you.

Turn to page 37.

"Hi sweetie, what are you doing up here?" Grandma asks. She snuck up on you, but she does that. Grandma is dressed in a beautiful black silk kimono and she holds a long silk scarf in her hands.

Then you hear a voice yelling for help from downstairs. "FIRE!! FIRE!! Get out of the building!"

What is going on with all of these emergencies? Something about the fire alarm sounds fake. But can you risk it?

If you tell Grandma Ami you think the jewel thieves are behind the door, and that you need help knocking it down, turn to page 42.

If you decide that a fire alarm is more important to investigate, turn to page 71.

You enter a scene of chaos. A fat mama raccoon and three baby raccoons are hissing and spitting from right beside the wedding cake. They've already chewed giant pieces away.

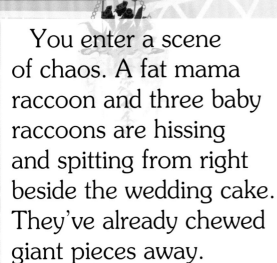

Turn to the next page.

What is left of the enormous cake stands on a cart in the far corner of the room. The seven layers of cake start from a bottom layer as big as a round lunch table. A baby raccoon stops hissing and calmly takes a bite out of the cake.

"Finally!" the pastry chef says, pointing a rolling pin at the raccoons. "I've been yelling about a raccoon alert for hours!"

Mama Raccoon licks her paws and makes a move toward the bottom layers of the cake. She gives you a low hiss like a whistle, but the baby raccoons look sleepy and nestle in for a snooze. They are actually really cute. Mama is still hungry and dives down a layer for some fresh cake.

"Not so fast," Grandma warns the raccoon. "Not on my watch!"

Grandma moves her arm in a swift downward motion and throws *shuriken*, or throwing stars, at the raccoon.

Go on to the next page.

THWUNK!

"Got ya!" Grandma Ami says.

The two front paws of the raccoon are secured to the pillars holding up the top layers of cake. The mama raccoon can't move, but she isn't hurt. She looks mad. The babies are snuffling and snoring.

"Now we have to get them out of here!" Grandma says.

Turn to the next page.

Later, after the raccoons are released in the wilderness, you look at the cake with Grandma Ami. The pastry chef removed the damaged layers, added new frosting, and set the miniature bride and groom on top of the cake. The bite marks are so small you can't see them from far away.

"What are we going to tell people about the cake?" you ask. "And where did those throwing stars come from?"

"It must have been the wind," Grandma says distractedly. "Don't worry, everything will be fine."

And it was.

The End

"I heard someone say they needed to keep a secret from Akiko," you tell Grandma Ami in a loud whisper. "I think they might be the ones who stole the jewels!"

"Okay," says Grandma Ami. She grabs the front of her kimono and gives it a twist, revealing purple ninja gear underneath. She pulls a mask over her head and breaks down the door.

You hear a crash and then, "Sweetie! Can you come help me?"

You scamper over the broken door to enter the room. Grandma, in her ninja gear, has pinned a man and a woman to the floor by standing on their shoulders! The woman is wearing workout clothes. She must be the person who knocked down the waiter! The man is wearing a sequined jacket and a fluorescent pink headband. You recognize him. He is Akiko's manager.

They try to wriggle away from Grandma, but she is too strong.

Turn to page 7.

"You can go," you tell the thief. "If you give me the case."

"Good," she says. "I'll leave the case here, move to the side and I'll be gone as quick as food from a bowl."

She nudges the case across the green grass. All is silent except for the rushing of the water far, far down below you.

Walking swiftly, but not running, the thief slips by you, turns a corner of the maze, and disappears.

You run for the case. Grandma and Grandpa won't be happy that you let the Jewel Ninja go, but they will be happy that you recovered the jewels in time for the wedding.

You pick up the briefcase by the handle, and it falls open. Empty!

"Oh, no!"

You've been tricked!

Turn to page 46.

You lunge for the jewel case as it sails through the air, but you don't reach it in time. The jewels will be lost in the river! A black grappling hook shoots out and snags the handle of the case.

The Jewel Ninja looks in surprise as the case is brought back.

"Fiddlesticks!" she says, before running away from the cliff.

"Trip her!" Grandpa PawPaw says as he reels the case with his grappling hook.

You stick out your foot, and *WHOOMP!* down she goes.

"Nice work, Young Adult Ninja!" Grandpa says. Your Baby Ninja days are finally over!

The End

What are you going to do? You turn around from the dead end and rush down one of the branches of the maze, but the Jewel Ninja is long gone.

"Hey, kiddo, heard you needed some help!" booms a familiar voice. "Any sign of the thief?"

It's Grandpa PawPaw, wearing a purple ninja outfit. He wears a floppy hat over his mask and he is holding a shovel like a staff.

You tell Grandpa what happened. He looks surprised but not angry.

"Don't worry, Snapdragon, you did the right thing. The Jewel Ninja is a strong adversary, and you wouldn't want to get into anything with her on your own."

"Thanks, PawPaw," you say. "But what are we going to do?"

Turn to page 13.

48

You decide to stay with Grandpa and help him get the reporters to leave.

"What do you know about Akiko's latest music video?" one of the reporters asks while you walk alongside them. Your grandpa herds them toward the gate.

"Sorry, folks, we don't know anything about it," Grandpa says.

The reporter who lost his camera heads out through the gate, but the spiky-haired reporter turns and runs back toward the inn! Grandpa bends down and lightly flicks a pebble at him. The pebble hits the running reporter in the back of the head. He stumbles to the ground. Grandpa winks at you.

"You okay, my friend?" Grandpa asks.

"Yeah," he says, slinking away.

"Private wedding, you understand. Now we must find your friend!" Grandpa says, then to you, "Let's go!"

Turn to page 50.

"Maybe we should find Grandma?" you ask. "I'm tired of running!"

"Toughen up, Snapdragon! We need to find that Jewel Ninja now. I'm worried she's heading to the gorge. Of course I want to get the jewels, but the main reason I'm worried is that she might get hurt. Lots of caves and sinkholes around there," Grandpa says, uncoiling a long silk rope from around his waist. "I see a footprint ahead. Come on. There she is!"

You can see the Jewel Ninja at the top of a ridge that leads to the river. She has ditched her reporter disguise and is wearing the dark blue bodysuit with the rip in it. By the time you get to the top she is gone, so you head down the path to the river. You reach a waterfall with a big, dark mouth of a cave behind it. Down below is a green pool of water. It is beautiful but loud.

Turn to page 70.

"I told you not to show anyone the veil!" says the bridesmaid wearing orange.

"Thanks for the reminder, Miko," Kioko answers. "Take the veil, get it to Akiko! We'll handle the Jewel Crew."

"Don't you want help?" you ask.

"No, just run," says Kioko, cracking her knuckles and doing a front flip down from the carriage.

Just as you are about to run with the veil, the ninja nearest you lifts her purple mask. It's Grandma! She winks at you and slips the mask back down. No one else saw. Maybe she wants you to stay?

If you decide to stay and help Grandma and the bridesmaids fight the Jewel Crew, turn to page 60.

If you run to bring Akiko her veil, turn to page 64.

You are brave enough to go into the cave behind the waterfall, even though it is dark and wet. You squeeze Grandpa's hand and he squeezes back. He shines a flashlight and you walk forward.

"Helloooo!" Grandpa yells, but the echo is the only answer. "Anyone in here?"

"This cave is huge," you say.

"It is a network of caves, and it goes on for miles," Grandpa tells you. "I used to explore a lot when we first moved here."

You are about to suggest going back to the light and warmth, when you hear people talking. There is a bright flash of light suddenly, and you can see the outlines of people standing in the cave. One of the people is very close to you, and he sees you. He looks like a giant wearing a suit. He comes right up to you.

"What are you doing here?" he booms at you.

Turn to page 56.

When your eyes clear, you see Akiko Yosano and her wedding party with her wedding photographer.

"Aren't caves cool?" Akiko asks, posing for the camera. "My photographer had the brilliant idea to take some wedding photos here in this magical cave."

There is another flash of light, and you see the Jewel Ninja in the background—sneaking away!

Grandpa moves to block the Jewel Ninja from escaping from the cave. Suddenly, they are in the air, trading blows and blocking them in rapid succession.

They are evenly matched, bouncing off the walls of the cave like ping-pong balls. The photographer snaps pictures furiously. You reach out and grab the Jewel Ninja's foot. She crashes to the ground, and you leap to catch the black velvet bag with the jewels! The wedding is saved.

The End

You decide to jump into the pool of water at the bottom of the falls. It is the only way to catch up with the thief.

"On the count of three, go!" says Grandpa, taking your hand. You jump off the ledge together and you fall in the center of the pool. Grandpa springs off a rock and backflips to land on his feet by the big rock.

"Wow, that was amazing," says the Jewel Ninja, lying on her back on a flat rock in the sun. "Wish I hadn't dropped the jewels when I jumped!"

"What do you mean? Where are the jewels?" Grandpa asks.

The Jewel Ninja points at the river. "Down there. Yeah, I think I'm done for the day," she says, sighing contentedly on her rock.

"We should get out of here if we want to get back in time for the wedding," he says to you.

"You see one wedding, you've seen them all," says the Jewel Ninja, closing her eyes.

The End

You aren't leaving Grandma alone, even if she does seem to be on the ninja team. You are sure she has her reasons.

"Prepare to be robbed!" threatens the Jewel Ninja, leaping toward the carriage.

"We're not pushovers," says Kioko. Miko nods in agreement.

The Jewel Ninja moves forward to grab Kioko, but she ducks and the Jewel Ninja misses.

Go on to the next page.

The other four, including Grandma, tighten their circle around the carriage. The horses stamp their feet nervously. The bridesmaids clump together. Just as the ninjas reach out to grab them, Grandma sweeps her leg beneath the Jewel Ninja's feet, grabbing another ninja's staff at the same time and using it to pin the Jewel Ninja to the ground.

Grandma then takes the *nunchucks* and trips the ninja holding the *sais* before bopping her on the head.

Turn to the next page.

"Let's get serious!" Grandma Ami says. "If you hand over the jewels now, I'll go easy on you."

The Jewel Ninja just laughs.

"Let's move this fight out in the open," Grandma says, pointing to a flat area.

"Fine," says the Jewel Ninja. "It will be a level playing field when I take you down, Ami-San. I've wanted this day to come for a long time."

Grandma Ami moves to the lawn and nods at the Jewel Ninja, pointing to a spot beneath a tree.

As soon as the Jewel Ninja reaches the spot, *WHAM!* a rope net traps her. She screams in rage and anger.

"You should know better than to fight a ninja on her home turf!" Grandma laughs.

Grandma takes off her mask and a huge smile spreads across her face. "Take me to that ceremony—I have some jewels to deliver. And then I want to dance!"

You and Grandma boogie over to the bride.

The End

You must bring the bride what she needs. Grandma Ami has a plan—you just don't know what it is.

"Prepare to fight!" says the Jewel Ninja, moving forward with her team.

"Oh, we'll fight!" says Kioko, doing a front flip onto the gravel driveway. The horses snort in surprise. "This wedding is so important I would fight an army of ninjas to make sure Akiko has her special day!"

The bridesmaids and the ninjas close in.

Suddenly Grandma is at your ear, and she whispers to you.

Go on to the next page.

"Get back to the inn! Go to the maze. The jewels are buried there, by the blue flamingo!"

Grandma slyly disrupts the fighting without the other ninjas noticing, keeping her disguise. Kioko uses surprising power to take on the Jewel Ninja. You dash to the carriage, veil in hand.

"Get us back to the inn!" you yell to Sophie, and she snaps the reins over the horses' backs so they take off running. You hold the veil tightly to you.

"Get the veil!" yells the Jewel Ninja, but it's too late. Sophie and the horses take you safely back to the inn.

The sounds of the battle fade as you reach the maze and step inside. Where is the blue flamingo? You know the maze by heart.

You rush through the maze, keeping an eye out for signs of fresh digging.

Turn to the next page.

There! Right by the fountain is a pile of fresh dirt! How could you have missed it before? You look up and see a blue flamingo over it. Of course. The famous flamingo fountain!

You dig with your bare hands, and almost immediately you feel something cold and hard. It's the tiara!

Grandma comes up behind you.

"We got her," Grandma tells you. "Thanks to the bridesmaids. Without their help I couldn't have taken on the whole Jewel Crew. That's why I was pretending to be one of them. A true ninja knows how to wait."

You pull up the tiara from the ground, feeling proud. But the tiara was buried straight in the ground, and there's dirt trapped in all of its crevices. It doesn't look nice. What are you going to do?

Turn to page 68.

"The show must go on!" says Akiko, holding the grubby tiara in her hands when you reach her back at the ceremony site. "Thank you for getting it, and the other jewels, back!" she says, kissing the top of your head. "Don't worry about the tiara. I think it looks cute with a little dirt, very earthy!"

The wedding is beautiful. Reo looks handsome in his tuxedo, and Akiko is beautiful in her white dress, even if her jewels have a little dirt on them. The bridesmaids are fresh from battle but they are happy and proud.

When the photos of the wedding are released to the tabloids, the "Dirty Jewelry Look" becomes a new fashion trend. Akiko even releases a new single, "A Dirty Crown (Is Better Than None)." It goes straight to number one on the charts!

The End

"Shoot!" Grandpa says. "I can't tell with all this mist where she scurried off to. Which way should we go? We'd have to jump, but it's a nice day for a swim!"

You look at the cave and think about how you are still a little bit afraid of the dark. Then you look at the pool of water below and think about how you are a little afraid of heights. And of rocks!

"Don't worry," Grandpa says, squeezing your hand. "I'll make sure you're okay. I honestly don't know which one to choose. I don't want her knocked out or lost in a dark hole, and if she did go down to the pool, she'll have a hard time getting out without a rope."

If you want to explore the dark cave behind the waterfall, turn to page 54.

If you decide to jump into the pool below, turn to page 58.

"Fire! Fire!" you hear the voice yelling. Then the fire alarm goes off: *whee-whoo, whee-whoo*. You know what's next because you've been at the inn for fire drills. You grit your teeth, tip back your head, and look up as the sprinklers turn on, showering you and Grandma with cold water.

"Look, there's smoke coming from the ballroom!" Grandma Ami says, pointing. "Come on!"

She leaps over the balcony upstairs and lands on her feet on the main floor. You take the stairs. Clouds of dark smoke come pouring out of the ballroom.

Grandma stands in the middle of the dance floor, holding up a trash can that has clouds of smoke coming from it.

"It's a diversion," she says calmly. "Someone set this fire. Can you open the doors to the patio, please, dear?"

Turn to the next page.

You open the doors and the smoke clears up. Why did someone set this fire?

The wedding is a huge success. You and Grandma Ami and Grandpa PawPaw dance until the moon comes up. The security team recovered the jewels in time. They were just being cleaned before the wedding, and the tent had been ripped when it was set up.

You don't learn why the fire was set until the next day, when photos of Akiko (and even you and Grandpa dancing) are the cover of *DailyWorldNewsInformer*. Someone set the fire and used the distraction to set up hidden cameras to get the photos, along with the million dollar payment. You never learn who those photographers were—maybe they were wedding guests, dancing alongside you?

The End

ABOUT THE AUTHOR

After graduating from Williams College with a degree specialization in ancient history, **Anson Montgomery** spent ten years founding and working in technology-related companies, as well as working as a freelance journalist for financial and local publications. He is the author of a number of books in the original *Choose Your Own Adventure* series, including *Everest Adventure, Snowboard Racer, Moon Quest* (reissued in 2008 by Chooseco), and  *CyberHacker* as well as two volumes of *Choose Your Own Adventure: The Golden Path.* Anson lives in Warren, Vermont, with his wife, Rebecca, and his two daughters, Avery and Lila.

ABOUT THE ARTIST

Keith Newton began his art career in the theater as a set painter. Having talent and a strong desire to paint portraits, he moved to New York and studied fine art at the Art Students League. Keith has won numerous awards in art such as The Grumbacher Gold Medallion and Salmagundi Award for Pastel. He soon began illustrating and was hired by Disney Feature Animation where he worked on such films as *Pocahontas*

 and *Mulan* as a background artist. Keith also designed color models for sculptures at Disney Animal Kingdom and has animated commercials for Euro Disney. Today, Keith Newton freelances from his home and teaches entertainment illustration at The College for Creative Studies in Detroit. He is married and has two daughters.

For games, activities, and other fun stuff, or to write to Anson Montgomery, visit us online at www.cyoa.com